His Essential Quotations

Delaplaine Essential Quotations

Editor - Andrew Delaplaine / Illustrator - Renee Delaplaine

Gramercy Park Press
New York – London - Paris

1.

We're born alone, we live alone, we die alone. Only through our love and friendship can we create the illusion for the moment that we're not alone.

2.

Create your own visual style…let it be unique for yourself and yet identifiable for others.

3.

Good evening, ladies and gentlemen. My name is Orson Welles. I am an actor. I am a writer. I am a director. I am a magician. I appear onstage and on the radio. Why are there so many of me and so few of you?

4.

If there hadn't been women we'd still be squatting in a cave eating raw meat, because we made civilization in order to impress our girlfriends.

5.
If you want a happy ending, that depends, of course, on where you stop your story.

6.
Nobody gets justice. People only get good luck or bad luck.

7.

Popularity should be no scale for the election of politicians. If it would depend on popularity, Donald Duck and The Muppets would take seats in the Senate.

8.

Personally, I don't like a girlfriend to have a husband. If she'll fool her husband, I figure she'll fool me.

9.

A film is never really good unless the camera is an eye in the head of a poet.

10.

In Italy, for 30 years under the Borgias, they had warfare, terror, murder and bloodshed, but they produced Michelangelo, Leonardo da Vinci and the Renaissance. In Switzerland they had brotherly love, they had 500 years of democracy and peace – and what did it produce? The cuckoo clock.

11.
Ask not what you can do for your
country. Ask what's for lunch.

12.

The classy gangster is a Hollywood invention.

13.

My doctor told me to stop having intimate dinners for four. Unless there are three other people.

14.

I was spoiled in a very strange way as a child, because everybody told me, from the moment I was able to hear, that I was absolutely marvelous, and I never heard a discouraging word for years, you see. I didn't know what was ahead of me.

15.
I have the terrible feeling that, because I am wearing a white beard and am sitting in the back of the theatre, you expect me to tell you the truth about something. These arc the cheap seats, not Mount Sinai.

16.
The notion of directing a film is the invention of critics – the whole eloquence of cinema is achieved in the editing room.

17.
I want to give the audience a hint of a scene. No more than that. Give them too much and they won't contribute anything themselves. Give them just a suggestion and you get them working with you. That's what gives the theatre meaning: when it becomes a social act.

18.
Everything about me is a contradiction, and so is everything about everybody else. We are made out of oppositions; we live between two poles. There's a philistine and an aesthete in all of us, and a murderer and a saint. You don't reconcile the poles. You just recognize them.

19.
The enemy of art is the absence of limitations.

20.
I have great love and respect for religion, great love and respect for atheism. What I hate is agnosticism, people who do not choose.

21.
A good artist should be isolated. If he isn't isolated, something is wrong.

22.
I know people who have a much better recollection of their childhood than I do. They remember very well when they were a year and a half and two years old. I've only one or two daguerreotypes that come to mind.

23.
Did you ever stop to think why cops are always famous for being dumb?
Simple. Because they don't have to be anything else.

24.
I have wasted the greater part of my life looking for money and trying to get along, trying to make my work from this terribly expensive paintbox, which is a movie. And I've spent too much energy on things that have nothing to do with making a movie. It's about two percent moviemaking and ninety-eight percent hustling. It's no way to spend a life.

25.
I've spent most of my mature life trying to prove that I'm not responsible.

26.
Living in the lap of luxury isn't bad
except that you never know when
luxury is going to stand up.

27.
Only very intelligent people don't wish
they were in politics, and I'm dumb
enough to want to be in there.

28.
I have always been more interested in
experiment, than in accomplishment.

29.
The essential is to excite the spectators.
If that means playing Hamlet on a flying
trapeze or in an aquarium, you do it.

30.

I'm never certain of a performance – my own or the other actors' – or the script or anything… But to me it seems there's only one place in the world the camera can be, and the decision usually comes immediately.

31.

I hate television. I hate it as much as peanuts. But I can't stop eating peanuts.

32.
Fake is as old as the Eden tree.

33.
I passionately hate the idea of being
with it; I think an artist has always to be
out of step with his time.

34.
Race hate isn't human nature; race hate
is the abandonment of human nature.

35.
Anybody who speaks quietly and
shrivels up in company is unbelievably
arrogant.

36.
Man is a rational animal who always
loses his temper when called upon to act
in accordance with the dictates of
reason.

37.

I'm one of those fellows so frightened
of driving that I go 80 miles an hour –
and the more frightened I get, the faster
I go.

38.

I don't pray because I don't want to
bore God.

39.

I feel I have to protect myself against
things. So I'm pretty careful to lose
most of them.

40.

I worry a lot about taking care of my
dependents, all those perfectly ordinary
middle-class preoccupations.

41.

Everybody denies I am a genius – but
nobody ever called me one!

42.
I don't like television when it gets near
to photographed plays.

43.

I hate Woody Allen physically, I dislike that kind of man.

44.

If everyone worked with wide-angled lenses, I'd shoot all my films in 75mm, because I believe very strongly in the possibilities of the 75mm.

45.

People are losing the capacity to listen to words or follow ideas.

46.

I have made an art form of the interview. The French are the best interviewers, despite their addiction to the triad, like all Cartesians.

47.

Ecstasy is not really part of the scene we can do on celluloid.

48.
Every actor in his heart believes
everything bad that's printed about him.

49.
I would rather be on the set than doing
anything.

50.
I do not suppose I shall be remembered
for anything. But I don't think about
my work in those terms. It is just as
vulgar to work for the sake of posterity
as to work for the sake of money.

51.
Criminals are never very amusing. It's
because they're failures. Those who
make real money aren't counted as
criminals. This is a class distinction,
not an ethical problem.

52.
I don't want to forgive myself. That's why I hate psychoanalysis. I think if you're guilty of something you should live with it. Get rid of it – how can you get rid of real guilt? I think people should live with it, face up to it.

53.
As a producer, sitting on the other side of the desk, I have never once had an agent go out on a limb for his client and fight for him. I've never heard one say, 'No, just a minute! This is the actor you should use.' They always say, 'You don't like him? I've got somebody else.' They're totally spineless.

54.
Each multiplex has screens allocated to each studio. The screens need filling. Studios have to create product to fill their screens, and the amount of good product is limited.

55.
I've never understood the cult of Hitchcock. Particularly the late American movies... Egotism and laziness. And they're all lit like television shows.

56.
The ideal American type is perfectly expressed by the Protestant, individualist, anti-conformist, and this is the type that is in the process of disappearing. In reality there are few left.

57.
I'm a provincial. I live very much like a hermit: reading, listening to music, working in the cutting room, writing, commercial work – which doesn't take up that much time.

58.
I think I made essential a mistake in staying in movies, because I – but it's a mistake I can't regret, because it's like saying, 'I shouldn't have stayed married to that woman, but I did because I love her.'

59.
When people accept breaking the law as normal, something happens to the whole society.

60.
They teach anything in universities today. You can major in mud pies.

61.
I have an unfortunate personality.

62.
The enemy of society is middle class and the enemy of life is middle age.

63.
Nobody who takes on anything big and tough can afford to be modest.

64.
I am essentially a hack, a commercial person. If I had a hobby, I would immediately make money on it or abandon it.

65.
There's no biography so interesting as the one in which the biographer is present.

66.
The first thing one must remember
about film is that it is a young medium.
And it is essential for every responsible
artist to cultivate the ground that has
been left fallow.

67.
In common with all Protestant or Jewish
culture, America was developed on the
idea that your word is your bond.
Otherwise, the frontier could have been
opened, 'cause it was lawless. A man's
word has to mean something.

68.
Now I'm an old Christmas tree, the root
of which have died. They must come
along and while the little needles fall off
me replace them with medallions.

69.
When you are down and out something always turns up – and it is usually the noses of your friends.

70.
I don't say we all ought to misbehave, but we ought to look as if we could.

71.
Gluttony is not a secret vice.

72.
My mother and father were both much more remarkable than any story of mine can make them. They seem to me just mythically wonderful.

73.
Hollywood is the only industry, even taking in soup companies, which does not have laboratories for the purpose of experimentation.

74.
I prefer the old masters, by which I mean John Ford, John Ford, and John Ford.

75.
Film is like a colony and there are very few colonists.

76.
Everything bad that has ever happened
to me has been caused by agents or
lawyers.

77.

'The Godfather' was the glorification of a bunch of bums who never existed.

78.

I never said I was a genius.

79.

My kind of director is an actor-director who writes.

80.

The two things you cannot do effectively on stage are pray and copulate.

81.

I have no great message to the world.

82.

When television came along, I'd already done more than 10 years of radio work and I thought everyone would want me. I sat around waiting for the phone to ring – and it didn't.

83.

I can think of nothing that an audience won't understand. The only problem is to interest them; once they are interested, they understand anything in the world.

84.

If you've noticed that I don't use long takes, it's not because I don't like them, but because no one gives me the necessary means to treat myself to them. It's more economical to make one image, then this image and then that image, and try to control them later, in the editing studio.

85.

I've always found it very sanitary to be broke.

86.

Now we sit through Shakespeare in order to recognize the quotations.

87.

Movie directing is a perfect refuge for the mediocre.

88.
One shouldn't ever be conscious of the author as lecturer. When social or moral points are too heavily stressed, I always get uncomfortable.

89.
The laws and the stage, both are a form of exhibitionism.

90.
There were centuries when civilization had no theater.

91.
See, I believe that it is not true that different races and nations are alike. I'm profoundly convinced that that's a total lie. I think people are different. Sardinians, for example, have stubby little fingers. Bosnians have short necks.

93.

In my real movie-going days, which were the thirties, you didn't stand in line. You strolled down the street and sallied into the theater at any hour of the day or night.

94.

Look at the real prodigies, and I look nothing compared to them.

95.
If I ever own a restaurant, I will never allow the waiters to ask if the diners like their dishes. Particularly when they're talking.

96.
The best thing commercially, which is the worst artistically, by and large, is the most successful.

97.
At twenty-one, so many things appear solid, permanent, untenable.

98.
On my tombstone, I want written: "He never did 'Love Boat'!"

99.
The only reason for doing a play is to make a statement about it, and by that I don't mean a conceit of the producer.

100.
I'm not a walking extra in a Chekov play; I'm no Slavic gloom or Irish gloom.

40131725R00025